MENTAL HEALTH, TRAUMA, AND THERAPY IN THE BLACK COMMUNITY

A JOURNEY FROM TRAUMA TO HEALING

J. CARTER HALE

DISCLAIMER

This book is for educational and informational purposes only. It is not psychotherapy, medical care, diagnosis, or legal advice, and it is not a substitute for treatment from a licensed mental health professional.

Some chapters discuss trauma, abuse, neglect, family violence, depression, suicidal ideation, and related themes that may be activating for some readers. Please move through the material at your own pace and seek support if needed.

If you are in immediate danger or in crisis, call or text 988 in the United States, contact local emergency services, or seek urgent help from a qualified crisis provider in your area.

AUTHOR'S NOTE

This book was written for readers who grew up in homes where pain was real but language for that pain was scarce. It is written for people who were told to be strong before they were ever taught how to be safe, honest, or emotionally seen.

The pages that follow bring together research, history, and lived patterns that are often recognized privately but rarely named publicly. The aim is not to pathologize Black families. The aim is to tell the truth about what survival has cost, what silence has protected, and what healing now requires.

Where the book names patterns, it does so to create clarity rather than blame. Where it offers hope, it does so without pretending that recovery is simple. The work of healing is demanding. It is also possible.

INTRODUCTION

This book examines childhood trauma, parental neglect, mental health stigma, and therapy barriers within the Black community. It argues that silence around suffering is not evidence of weakness or indifference. It is often the inheritance of generations who were forced to survive without emotional safety, without language for distress, and without reliable access to care.

The chapters that follow draw on peer-reviewed research, public-health data, and historical context to name recurring wounds: adverse childhood experiences, fear-based parenting, emotional neglect, father absence, step-family conflict, witnessed violence, chronic rage, and the burden of performing strength. Throughout, the goal is not only to explain injury but to point toward healing.

The central claim is simple: the Black community's relationship to mental health treatment is not a personal failing. It is shaped by history, mistrust, scarcity, and deeply learned survival strategies. What was learned can be named. What is named can be confronted. And what is confronted can begin to heal.

PART I

THE LANDSCAPE OF SILENCE

1

MENTAL HEALTH STIGMA IN THE BLACK COMMUNITY

DEFINING THE PROBLEM

Mental health stigma is the set of negative beliefs, attitudes, and social consequences attached to mental illness and treatment-seeking. Within the Black community, stigma operates on multiple levels simultaneously — individual shame, family disapproval, community judgment, and cultural narrative — creating a multi-layered barrier that prevents millions of Black Americans from accessing care they urgently need.

Understanding this stigma requires understanding its origins. It did not emerge from weakness or ignorance. It emerged from survival.

WHAT THE RESEARCH SHOWS

The treatment gap between Black and white Americans is one of the most persistent and well-documented disparities in American healthcare:

Only 31% of Black adults with a diagnosable mental illness receive treatment, compared to 48% of white adults — a gap of 17 percentage points that has remained largely unchanged for two decades (Substance Abuse and Mental Health Services Administration [SAMHSA], 2023).

Black children are less likely to receive mental and behavioral health services than white children, even when presenting with comparable need (Hoffmann et al., 2022).

An estimated 68% of Black Americans live in federally designated mental health professional shortage areas, meaning geographic access — before stigma is even a factor — is already severely constrained (Health Resources and Services Administration [HRSA], 2022).

Mental health stigma, distrust of institutions, cost, and provider scarcity remain recurring barriers to care in Black communities.

THE ROOTS OF STIGMA: A SYSTEMIC READING

The cultural emphasis on "strength" and self-reliance within Black communities does not exist in a vacuum. It is a direct inheritance of slavery, during which Black people were denied the right to grieve, to break down, or to be seen as fully human. Emotional suppression was not a character flaw — it was a survival mechanism. To cry in public was dangerous. To be labeled "unstable" was to lose what little autonomy existed.

Four overlapping forces sustain stigma today:

1. Historical mistrust of medical institutions — rooted in documented abuses including the Tuskegee Syphilis Study, forced sterilizations, and the consistent undertreatment of Black pain (Washington, 2006).

2. Cultural emphasis on strength and self-reliance — the "Strong Black woman/man" archetype, explored in depth in Chapter Nine of this manuscript.

3. Religious and spiritual frameworks — the phrase "pray it away" reflects a genuine faith tradition, not ignorance, though it becomes problematic when used to deny access to clinical care.

4. Lack of culturally competent providers — only 4% of American psychologists identify as Black or African American (American Psychological Association [APA], 2021), creating a structural barrier to culturally resonant care.

THE COST OF SILENCE: PREVENTION VS. INTERVENTION

When stigma prevents early treatment, the consequences compound:

Early identification and treatment can improve long-term outcomes and reduce the chance that distress becomes more deeply entrenched over time.

Untreated childhood trauma significantly elevates risk across multiple domains:

Depression: 5x higher risk

Anxiety disorders: 4x higher risk

PTSD: 6x higher risk

Substance abuse: 3x higher risk

Suicidal ideation: 7x higher risk

(Felitti et al., 1998; Substance Abuse and Mental Health Services Administration, 2023)

The silence is not free. It has a price — and the Black community has been paying it for generations.

2

ADVERSE CHILDHOOD EXPERIENCES (ACES) AND LONG-TERM IMPACT

WHAT ARE ACES?

Adverse Childhood Experiences (ACEs) are potentially traumatic events that occur before the age of 18. The landmark CDC-Kaiser Permanente ACE Study, which began in 1995 and published its foundational findings in 1998, surveyed more than 17,000 adults and established that childhood trauma is not only common — it is the single strongest predictor of adult health outcomes across virtually every domain (Felitti et al., 1998).

Important research context: While the original ACE Study remains the most cited work in this field, subsequent researchers have raised important critiques, including the study's original sample being predominantly white, middle-class, and insured. A growing body of updated ACE research — including community-based studies by the CDC and the Robert Wood Johnson Foundation — has expanded and refined these findings across racial and socioeconomic groups (Merrick et al., 2018; Wade et al., 2014).

The ten recognized ACE categories are:

Abuse

1. Physical abuse

2. Emotional abuse
3. Sexual abuse

Neglect

4. Physical neglect
5. Emotional neglect

Household Dysfunction

6. Witnessing domestic violence
7. Household substance abuse
8. Household mental illness
9. Parental separation or divorce
10. Incarcerated household member

THE NUMBERS: CUMULATIVE RISK

ACEs do not operate in isolation — they accumulate, and each additional ACE compounds risk exponentially:

64% of all U.S. adults have experienced at least one ACE (Centers for Disease Control and Prevention [CDC], 2023).

40% of Black children experience two or more ACEs, compared to 29% of white children — a disparity directly linked to economic inequality, neighborhood segregation, and systemic racism (Merrick et al., 2018).

With each additional ACE, risk of negative outcome increases:

Depression: 20–30% increased risk per ACE

Suicide attempt: 60% increased risk per ACE

Chronic health problems: 50% increased risk per ACE

Adults with four or more ACEs face dramatically elevated lifetime risk:

4x more likely to develop depression

12x more likely to attempt suicide

10x more likely to inject drugs

2.5x more likely to develop chronic disease

(Felitti et al., 1998; Merrick et al., 2018)

WHY BLACK CHILDREN CARRY A HEAVIER ACE BURDEN

The disproportionate ACE exposure among Black children is not a cultural phenomenon. It is a policy outcome. Decades of redlining concentrated Black families in under-resourced neighborhoods. Mass incarceration removed fathers and mothers from homes at catastrophic rates. Wage gaps generated the economic stress that strains even the most loving households. The ACE burden is the ledger of systemic racism — written into the bodies and nervous systems of children who had no hand in creating it.

PART II

WHAT HAPPENED IN THE HOUSE

3

PARENTING PATTERNS AND GENERATIONAL TRAUMA

UNDERSTANDING AUTHORITARIAN PARENTING IN CONTEXT

Authoritarian parenting — characterized by high demands, strict discipline, low warmth, and limited explanation — appears at higher rates in Black families than in white families in available research. This finding requires careful contextual reading before any interpretation is applied.

Research indicates:

Strict, fear-based parenting patterns appear in many Black families, but the story is more complex than a single percentage can capture.

Critical context: Classic parenting-style research distinguishes authoritarian parenting from authoritative parenting by the balance of control, warmth, and responsiveness (Baumrind, 1991; Lamborn et al., 1991). In Black family life, however, strictness has often been shaped by danger, scarcity, and the felt need to prepare children for a hostile world. That history does not make harshness harmless. It does help explain why some patterns survived.

Contributing factors to authoritarian parenting patterns in Black families:

Internalized survival mechanisms passed from enslaved ancestors who had to raise children to survive a brutal system

Economic stress and the cognitive load of single-parent households

Cultural transmission across generations with no access to parenting education

Structural lack of family support services in Black communities

IMPACT ON CHILDREN

Fear-based parenting, regardless of its survival origins, creates measurable psychological consequences in children:

Reduced self-esteem and confidence in autonomous decision-making

Difficulty setting and maintaining personal boundaries

Poor emotional regulation — because emotions were not modeled, named, or validated

Elevated rates of anxiety and depression in adolescence and adulthood

Strained parent-child relationships that persist into adulthood

(Gershoff & Grogan-Kaylor, 2016)

THE INFALLIBILITY BARRIER

A recurring dynamic in authoritarian households is what this manuscript terms the Infallibility Barrier: the cultural prohibition against parents acknowledging error. When a parent operates as though they are incapable of being wrong, the household becomes a closed system in which:

Children fear sharing problems because there is no safe space for them to exist as imperfect beings

Communication flows in one direction — from authority downward

Emotional needs are consistently invalidated as weakness or disobedience

A child's developing autonomy is systematically suppressed

4

EMOTIONAL NEGLECT AND PSYCHOLOGICAL IMPACT

WHAT EMOTIONAL NEGLECT LOOKS LIKE

Emotional neglect is among the most underacknowledged forms of childhood trauma — precisely because it is defined by absence rather than action. It leaves no visible marks. It can coexist with material provision. And it is frequently invisible to the very parents who are perpetuating it, because they, too, were emotionally neglected.

Forms of emotional neglect include:

Absence of verbal affirmation — children who never heard "I love you," "I'm proud of you," or "I believe in you"

Absence of physical comfort — no hugs, no physical reassurance during distress

Emotional unavailability — a parent who is physically present but psychologically absent

Chronic invalidation — responses to a child's emotional expression that dismiss, minimize, or punish feeling

RESEARCH FINDINGS

Emotional neglect is often hidden beneath provision, discipline, and duty. In many homes, love may be present but still go largely unspoken, unmodeled, or emotionally untranslated.

Across the trauma literature, emotional neglect is associated with lasting psychological harm, including:

Higher rates of adult depression

Increased anxiety and chronic hypervigilance

Relationship difficulties, including chronic difficulty trusting partners

Persistent shame, abandonment fear, and feelings of unworthiness that can remain active for years if left unaddressed

THE SECONDARY WOUNDS

Emotional neglect rarely exists alone. It is typically accompanied by:

Comparison and Scapegoating: Being held to different standards than siblings; being labeled the "problem child" or "black sheep"; being blamed for family dysfunction that originated with the adults around them.

Hypocrisy in the Parent-Child Relationship: Parents who were emotionally or physically absent during childhood later demanding emotional closeness, financial support, or caregiving from adult children — using manipulation, guilt, or the performance of crisis to extract what was never given.

PSYCHOLOGICAL CONSEQUENCES

Adults who experienced emotional neglect in childhood commonly present with:

Profound difficulty trusting others — because trust was never modeled as safe

People-pleasing behaviors — because approval was conditional and unpredictable

Inability to set or maintain healthy boundaries — because boundaries were never respected

Oscillation between perfectionism and self-sabotage

A chronic underlying sense of being a "burden" — of taking up too much space

These are not personality traits. They are adaptations. And adaptations can be unlearned.

5

ABSENT PARENTS AND THE FATHER-SHAPED WOUND

THE DATA ON PARENTAL ABSENCE

Father absence in Black families is among the most politically weaponized statistics in American public discourse. It is used to pathologize Black culture, to deflect from systemic causes, and to place the weight of policy failure on individual Black men. Any honest engagement with this data requires refusing that framing while still acknowledging the real wound that absence creates in a child.

Current national data show that Black children are disproportionately likely to live in single-parent households:

Roughly two-thirds of Black children live in single-parent households (The Annie E. Casey Foundation, 2022; U.S. Census Bureau, 2023).

The causes of this reality are overwhelmingly structural:

Black men were imprisoned at 5.5 times the rate of white men in 2021 — a mass removal from families shaped by racially unequal policing, prosecution, and sentencing (Ghandnoosh, 2023).

Economic instability, generational poverty, and lack of family support infrastructure compound the crisis

Historical systemic racism has systematically disrupted Black family formation across every generation since slavery

THE IMPACT ON CHILDREN

Children without consistent paternal involvement show elevated risk across multiple domains:

2x higher school dropout rates

3x higher rates of behavioral difficulties

4x higher rates of childhood poverty

5x higher incarceration rates among boys

(McLanahan & Sandefur, 1994; The Annie E. Casey Foundation, 2022)

These outcomes are not inevitable. They are the statistical consequence of raising children in systems designed to fail them, without the resources those children need.

THE COMPARISON WOUND

A child growing up without a father does not suffer primarily in the abstract. The wound becomes concrete in daily moments: watching a friend's father attend a school play, a classmate's dad teaching him to drive, a peer's father walking her to prom. These ordinary moments become extraordinary evidence of an absence that feels personal — even when its causes are entirely systemic.

This experience creates a specific emotional injury: the belief that one was not worth staying for. That belief, if unaddressed, shapes attachment patterns, romantic relationships, and parenting behavior across the remainder of a life.

6

BLENDED FAMILY TRAUMA AND STEP-PARENT DYNAMICS

THE RESEARCH ON STEP-FAMILY CONFLICT

Blended family formation — increasingly common across all demographics — introduces a complex set of loyalty conflicts, boundary questions, and authority struggles that can become genuinely traumatic for children when navigated poorly.

Research findings:

42% of children in step-families report significant ongoing conflict (Sweeney, 2010; Pew Research Center, 2011)

Step-mothers are statistically more likely than step-fathers to experience conflict with step-children — a finding researchers connect to differential gender expectations around nurturing (Ganong & Coleman, 2017)

Biological parent loyalty conflict — a parent caught between a new partner and their child — is among the most consistently identified predictors of poor step-family outcomes

PATTERNS OF DYSFUNCTION IN STEP-FAMILY SYSTEMS

Research on step-family conflict identifies several recurring dynamics that, at their most severe, constitute emotional abuse:

Triangulation: A step-parent who works through the biological parent to control, criticize, or punish the child rather than engaging directly

Gaslighting: Convincing a child that their experience of mistreatment is distorted ("you're too sensitive," "that never happened")

Isolation tactics: Systematically undermining the child's relationship with the biological parent

Scapegoating: Making the step-child the identified source of household conflict

COMPLEX PTSD: A NOTE ON DIAGNOSIS

Children raised in chronically unsafe households — including those characterized by step-parent abuse and biological parent non-protection — frequently develop Complex PTSD (C-PTSD), which is distinct from standard PTSD in important ways.

While standard PTSD typically follows a single traumatic event, C-PTSD develops from prolonged, repeated trauma — particularly in childhood, and particularly when the perpetrators are caregivers from whom escape is impossible. Symptoms include:

Difficulty regulating emotions

Persistent negative self-perception ("I am damaged," "I am worthless")

Difficulty sustaining relationships

Altered consciousness (dissociation, emotional numbing)

Loss of meaning or hope

C-PTSD is increasingly recognized by trauma clinicians (Herman, 1992; van der Kolk, 2014) and is recognized in the ICD-11 diagnostic system (World Health Organization, 2019), though it remains absent from the DSM-5. This gap itself reflects the way diagnostic systems have historically underserved populations whose trauma is chronic and relational rather than acute and event-based.

7

DOMESTIC VIOLENCE, WITNESSED VIOLENCE, AND THE BODY'S MEMORY

WHAT THE DATA SHOWS

Witnessing violence between caregivers is itself a form of childhood trauma — one that the original ACE Study counted as a separate adverse experience, distinct from being directly abused.

Between 15–20% of American children witness domestic violence in any given year (Centers for Disease Control and Prevention [CDC], 2020)

Black children are disproportionately exposed to intimate partner violence because structural inequities intensify housing instability, economic stress, and caregiver burden.

EFFECTS OF WITNESSING PARENTAL VIOLENCE

Children who witness violence between caregivers experience:

Chronic hypervigilance — a nervous system permanently scanning for threat

Learned conflict resolution patterns — the internalization of aggression or submission as the only available responses to disagreement

Normalization of violence — a recalibrated threshold for what relationships are supposed to feel like

Protective role parentification — children who physically intervene in adult violence are robbed of childhood and carry the weight of an impossibly adult responsibility

LONG-TERM CONSEQUENCES IN ADULTHOOD

Adults who witnessed childhood domestic violence show significantly elevated lifetime risk:

3x more likely to perpetrate intimate partner violence

4x more likely to become victims of intimate partner violence

6x more likely to develop PTSD

Higher rates of substance abuse, depression, and anxiety disorders

(Krug et al., 2002; Abramsky et al., 2011)

This is not destiny. It is pattern — and patterns can be interrupted. But interruption requires that the pattern first be named.

PART III

WHAT WE CARRY

8

RAGE, INTERNALIZED ANGER, AND THE MYTH OF "GETTING OVER IT"

THE RAGE RESPONSE: WHAT CHRONIC TRAUMA DOES TO ANGER

Prolonged abuse — particularly by caregivers, in spaces that were supposed to be safe — produces a specific emotional residue in survivors. It is not ordinary anger. It is a rage that has nowhere to go: it cannot be expressed toward the perpetrator (who holds power), it cannot be released (because the environment remains unsafe), and it cannot be discharged through the usual outlets of grievance and repair.

This unprocessed rage accumulates. It turns inward. And when it turns outward — in adulthood, in relationships, in traffic, in moments of perceived disrespect — it often confuses and frightens the survivor themselves.

WHAT RESEARCH SHOWS ABOUT CHRONIC ANGER

Unprocessed trauma-based anger is not a character flaw. It is a physiological state with measurable health consequences:

Chronic anger is associated with 2x higher risk of cardiovascular disease (Chida & Steptoe, 2009)

Persistent anger and hostility predict higher rates of depression, anxiety, and relationship dissolution

Trauma-based rage is frequently misdirected — expressed toward safe relationships while the original wound remains untouched

(Novaco, 2011; van der Kolk, 2014)

THE DESIRE FOR JUSTICE IS NORMAL

It is important to name something that therapy sometimes fails to honor: the desire for acknowledgment, accountability, and justice from people who harmed you is not pathological. It is human. The fantasy of confrontation, of making someone understand what they did, of watching them face consequences — these are not symptoms of a diseased mind. They are the mind's attempt to resolve what was never resolved.

The therapeutic work is not to eliminate that desire but to understand it — to stop waiting for an apology that may never come, and to locate justice within the self rather than in the perpetrator's response.

9

THE STRENGTH MYTH — SUPERWOMAN, SUPERMAN, AND THE COST OF NEVER BREAKING DOWN

NAMING THE WOUND

No section of this manuscript requires more space than this one — because no wound in the Black community is more invisible, more celebrated, or more lethal.

The "Strong Black woman" and "Strong Black man" archetypes are not compliments. They are cages. They are the cultural inheritance of a system that needed Black people to endure without complaint — and that found a way to make endurance feel like identity, like pride, like the thing that makes you you.

But you cannot be strong all the time. No human being can. And when the culture around you has no language for your breakdown — when vulnerability is equated with weakness, when crying is equated with giving up, when asking for help is read as failure — the only available option is to hold it in. And hold it in. And hold it in.

Until the body decides for you.

THE RESEARCH: SUPERWOMAN SCHEMA

Psychologist Cheryl Woods-Giscombé coined the term Superwoman Schema (SWS) to describe the constellation of beliefs and behaviors that define the Strong Black Woman archetype (Woods-Giscombé, 2010). Her qualitative research with Black women identified five core components:

1. Obligation to project strength — regardless of actual internal state
2. Obligation to suppress emotions — particularly "negative" emotions like sadness, fear, or neediness
3. Resistance to being vulnerable or appearing vulnerable to others, including intimate partners
4. Obligation to help others — placing family and community needs consistently above personal needs
5. Perceived sense of duty to succeed — the belief that Black women cannot afford to fail, because the stakes for their families and communities are too high

These five components produce a specific and measurable set of health consequences.

THE PHYSICAL COST OF THE STRENGTH MYTH

The body is not a metaphor. When emotions are chronically suppressed, the physiological systems designed to process stress — the hypothalamic-pituitary-adrenal axis, the inflammatory response, the cardiovascular system — do not stop working. They keep working. They work overtime. And eventually, they break.

Research linking emotional suppression and chronic stress to physical health outcomes in Black women is substantial:

Chronic stress is increasingly recognized as one pathway linking racism, emotional suppression, and hypertension in Black women (Sims et al., 2012).

Weathering — the hypothesis that Black Americans age faster biologically due to the cumulative stress of racism — was first described by Arline Geronimus in 1992 and has since been supported by research on telomere length and epigenetic aging markers

Black women have among the highest rates of allostatic load (the biological wear-and-tear of chronic stress) of any demographic group in the United States (Geronimus et al., 2006)

THE PARALLEL WOUND IN BLACK MEN

For Black men, the strength myth operates through a parallel but distinct mechanism. The cultural prohibition against male vulnerability — intensified within Black communities by the additional pressure of navigating a world that already perceives Black men as threatening — creates a specific trap:

Black men are expected to be strong in the face of racism. They are expected to be strong in the face of poverty. They are expected to be strong in the face of violence. And when they break — when the weight of all of that becomes unbearable — the breakdown is read as weakness, as failure, as loss of manhood.

The result is a catastrophic underutilization of mental health services. Black men are among the least likely demographic groups to seek therapy — not because they suffer least, but because the cultural permission to suffer openly does not exist for them.

INTERGENERATIONAL TRANSMISSION

The strength myth does not exist in isolation — it is transmitted. Parents who learned to suppress their own pain teach their children, explicitly and implicitly, to suppress theirs:

A mother who never cried in front of her children teaching them that tears are weakness

A father who worked through illness because rest was not something he was ever allowed to model

A family system where "we don't air our business" means no one ever gets the language for what happened to them

This is how trauma travels. Not through weakness. Through the exact opposite of weakness — through the heroic, exhausting, ultimately self-defeating commitment to appearing fine.

TOWARD A NEW DEFINITION OF STRENGTH

True strength is not the suppression of pain. It is the willingness to face pain — to name it, to carry it to a therapist's office, to sit with it until it loses its power over you. It is the parent who breaks the cycle by telling their child "I love you" for the first time, even when no one ever said it to them. It is the survivor who chooses therapy over performance.

That is strength. And it looks nothing like what we were taught.

(See Woods-Giscombé, 2010; Beauboeuf-Lafontant, 2009; Geronimus et al., 2006; Wallace & Constantine, 2005.)

PART IV

THE WORK OF HEALING

10

HISTORICAL TRAUMA — THE WOUND WE INHERITED

INTERGENERATIONAL TRAUMA: WHAT THE RESEARCH SHOWS

The concept of intergenerational — or historical — trauma holds that the psychological effects of extreme collective trauma do not end with the generation that experienced them. They are transmitted to subsequent generations through a combination of behavioral modeling, altered parenting patterns, institutional distrust, and — increasingly — biological mechanisms.

Evidence for intergenerational trauma transmission comes from multiple research traditions:

Psychological and behavioral transmission:

Research on Holocaust survivors and their children has consistently demonstrated elevated rates of PTSD, anxiety, and dysregulated stress response in the second generation — people who did not personally experience the Holocaust but inherited its psychological signature (Yehuda et al., 2016)

Analogous patterns have been documented in descendants of enslaved people, Japanese American internment camp survivors, and Native American boarding school survivors

Epigenetic transmission:

Emerging research in epigenetics — the study of how environmental experiences alter gene expression without changing DNA sequence — suggests that trauma can produce heritable biological changes (Yehuda et al., 2016; Bowers & Yehuda, 2016)

Important caveat: Epigenetic research in humans is still early-stage, and its application to intergenerational trauma remains scientifically contested. The field is promising but should be cited with appropriate precision — "emerging evidence suggests" rather than "research proves." Overstating this claim invites legitimate scientific challenge.

HISTORICAL ROOTS OF TRAUMA IN BLACK AMERICA

The historical sources of collective trauma in the Black community are not abstract. They are documented:

Slavery: The systematic destruction of African family structures, cultural identity, language, and kinship — a 246-year project of dehumanization that included the routine separation of children from parents at auction

Reconstruction and Jim Crow: The violent suppression of Black political, economic, and social advancement through lynching, convict leasing, and legal apartheid

Redlining and economic exclusion: Federal housing policies that deliberately concentrated Black families in under-resourced areas, denying them the generational wealth-building available to white families

Mass incarceration: The explosion of Black imprisonment following the 1970s — documented in Michelle Alexander's The New Jim Crow and later sentencing research — representing a modern extension of family separation as policy (Alexander, 2010; Ghandnoosh, 2023)

These are not talking points. They are the causal chain that connects historical policy to present-day mental health disparities.

SURVIVAL-BASED PARENTING

Authoritarian parenting norms in Black families cannot be understood outside this historical context. Enslaved parents who loved their children deeply had to prepare them for brutality — and warmth, in that context, was a luxury that could get a child killed. The transmission of harsh discipline across generations is not a cultural preference. It is a survival strategy that outlived the conditions that made it necessary — and is now causing harm in the very families it was designed to protect.

11

EVIDENCE-BASED PATHWAYS TO HEALING

WHY THERAPY WORKS — AND WHY IT'S NOT "WEAKNESS"

Therapy is not a last resort. It is not what you do when you have completely fallen apart. It is preventive medicine for the most complex organ in the human body — the mind — and the most sophisticated system we possess for navigating the world: the nervous system.

Therapy works because it does something no other relationship can do: it provides a structured, boundaried space in which a trained professional helps you understand the patterns you developed in order to survive — and develop new patterns designed for thriving.

Evidence-based approaches with established efficacy for trauma:

Trauma-Focused Cognitive Behavioral Therapy (TF-CBT)

Specifically designed for children and adolescents who have experienced trauma, with a parallel component for caregivers

Demonstrates significant reduction in PTSD symptoms, depression, and behavioral difficulties

The research base is robust and replicated across multiple studies and populations

(Cohen et al., 2017; National Child Traumatic Stress Network, 2024)

EMDR (Eye Movement Desensitization and Reprocessing)

Developed by Francine Shapiro; extensively validated for PTSD

WHO-recommended treatment for PTSD in adults and children

Particularly effective for discrete traumatic memories and trauma-related intrusive symptoms

(World Health Organization, 2013; van den Berg et al., 2015)

Family Systems Therapy

Addresses the relational and generational patterns from which individual trauma emerges

Particularly valuable for breaking cycles of dysfunction across generations

Murray Bowen's foundational work on intergenerational transmission is directly relevant to the Black family experience (Bowen, 1978).

Group Therapy and Community-Based Healing

Reduces isolation and shame through shared witness

Culturally, community has always been central to Black healing — group modalities that harness this are particularly powerful

Peer support groups, church-based mental health initiatives, and community healing circles all draw on this tradition

NAVIGATING CULTURALLY COMPETENT CARE

Not all therapy is created equal. A therapist who does not understand the Black experience — who pathologizes survival strategies, who is unfamiliar with the history of medical racism, who cannot hold the complexity of code-switching, microaggression, and structural oppression — can do active harm.

Finding culturally competent care matters. The support guide in the back matter includes directories of Black therapists and culturally responsive mental health organizations.

12

BREAKING THE CYCLE — A CALL TO ACTION

FOR PARENTS

Breaking the cycle does not require perfection. It requires intention — and the willingness to do something your own parents may never have done: acknowledge that you are fallible, that your children have needs you may have missed, and that it is never too late to repair a relationship.

Six commitments for parents who want to break the cycle:

1. Admit imperfection openly — Model healthy accountability. When you are wrong, say so. Your children do not need you to be infallible. They need you to be honest.

2. Create genuine open communication — Not the performance of openness, but the actual practice of listening without punishment.

3. Express love explicitly — Say it. Show it. Regularly. Unconditionally.

4. Actively support your children's dreams — Not the dreams you chose for them, but the ones they carry.

5. Balance discipline with dignity — You can hold firm limits without humiliation, fear, or violence.

6. Seek help together — Family therapy is not an admission of failure. It is a decision to do better — together.

FOR SURVIVORS

You did not choose what happened to you. You were a child. The responsibility for what occurred in your childhood rests with the adults who were supposed to protect you — not with you.

Five truths for survivors:

1. Your trauma is valid — regardless of whether your family acknowledges it, regardless of whether you can "prove" it, regardless of whether your experience was "worse" than someone else's.

2. It was not your fault — not even the parts you have convinced yourself were your fault.

3. Healing is possible — not the erasure of what happened, but a life in which what happened does not run everything.

4. You deserve love — unconditional, consistent, patient love. Including from yourself.

5. You can parent differently — the cycle can end with you. Many survivors have ended it. You can too.

SUPPORT AND RESOURCE GUIDE

IMMEDIATE CRISIS SUPPORT

• 988 Suicide & Crisis Lifeline — Free 24/7 crisis support by call, text, or chat. Call/text: 988. Web: 988lifeline.org/get-help.

• SAMHSA National Helpline — Free, confidential 24/7 treatment referral and information service in English and Spanish. Call: 1-800-662-HELP (4357). Web: samhsa.gov/find-help/helplines.

• Crisis Text Line — Free 24/7 text-based crisis support. Text: HOME to 741741. Web: crisistextline.org.

BLACK MENTAL HEALTH RESOURCES

• Black Mental Health Alliance — Culturally relevant education, advocacy, referral support, and community resources. Web: blackmentalhealth.com.

• Therapy for Black Girls — Therapist directory and mental health resources for Black women and girls. Web: providers.therapyforblackgirls.com.

• Therapy for Black Men — Therapist directory and support

resources focused on Black men and boys. Web: therapyforblackmen.org.

• Boris Lawrence Henson Foundation — Community resources and culturally relevant mental wellness programs. Web: borislhensonfoundation.org/resources.

GENERAL MENTAL HEALTH RESOURCES

• NAMI HelpLine — Non-crisis emotional support, mental health information, and referrals. Call/text: 1-800-950-NAMI (6264) or NAMI to 62640. Web: nami.org/help.

• Psychology Today Therapist Directory — Search by specialty, insurance, location, and therapist identity. Web: psychologytoday.com/us/therapists.

• Open Path Psychotherapy Collective — Lower-cost therapy network for individuals, couples, and families. Web: openpathcollective.org/find-a-therapist.

LOWER-COST CARE OPTIONS

• **Community mental health centers:** Many offer sliding-scale services funded through local or state systems.

• **University training clinics:** Supervised graduate clinicians may provide lower-cost therapy.

• **Employee Assistance Programs (EAPs):** Some employers provide short-term counseling at no cost.

• **Medicaid and state programs:** Coverage varies by state but often includes behavioral health services.

BIBLIOGRAPHY

Abramsky, T., Watts, C. H., Garcia-Moreno, C., Devries, K., Kiss, L., Ellsberg, M., ... & Heise, L. (2011). What factors are associated with recent intimate partner violence? Findings from the WHO multi-country study on women's health and domestic violence. BMC Public Health, 11(1), 109.

Alexander, M. (2010). The New Jim Crow: Mass incarceration in the age of colorblindness. The New Press.

American Psychological Association. (2021). Demographic characteristics of APA members by membership category. APA Center for Workforce Studies.

Baumrind, D. (1991). The influence of parenting style on adolescent competence and substance use. The Journal of Early Adolescence, 11(1), 56–95.

Beauboeuf-Lafontant, T. (2009). Behind the mask of the strong Black woman: Voice and the embodiment of a costly performance. Temple University Press.

Bowen, M. (1978). Family therapy in clinical practice. Jason Aronson.

Bowers, M. E., & Yehuda, R. (2016). Intergenerational transmission of stress in humans. Neuropsychopharmacology, 41(1), 232–244.

Centers for Disease Control and Prevention. (2020). Preventing intimate partner violence. National Center for Injury Prevention and Control.

Centers for Disease Control and Prevention. (2023). Adverse childhood experiences (ACEs): Preventing early trauma to improve adult health. Division of Violence Prevention.

Chida, Y., & Steptoe, A. (2009). The association of anger and hostility with future coronary heart disease: A meta-analytic review of prospective evidence. Journal of the American College of Cardiology, 53(11), 936–946.

Cohen, J. A., Mannarino, A. P., & Deblinger, E. (2017). Treating trauma and traumatic grief in children and adolescents (2nd ed.). Guilford Press.

Felitti, V. J., Anda, R. F., Nordenberg, D., Williamson, D. F., Spitz, A. M., Edwards, V., Koss, M. P., & Marks, J. S. (1998). Relationship of childhood abuse and household dysfunction to many of the leading causes of death in adults: The Adverse Childhood Experiences (ACE) study. American Journal of Preventive Medicine, 14(4), 245–258.

Ganong, L., & Coleman, M. (2017). Stepfamily relationships: Development, dynamics, and interventions (2nd ed.). Springer.

Geronimus, A. T., Hicken, M., Keene, D., & Bound, J. (2006). "Weathering" and age patterns of allostatic load scores among Blacks and whites in the United States. American Journal of Public Health, 96(5), 826–833.

Gershoff, E. T., & Grogan-Kaylor, A. (2016). Spanking and child outcomes: Old controversies and new meta-analyses. Journal of Family Psychology, 30(4), 453–469.

Ghandnoosh, N. (2023). One in five: Ending racial inequity in incarceration. The Sentencing Project.

Health Resources and Services Administration. (2022). Designated health professional shortage areas statistics. Bureau of Health Workforce.

Herman, J. L. (1992). Trauma and recovery: The aftermath of violence — from domestic abuse to political terror. Basic Books.

Hoffmann, J. A., Alegría, M., Alvarez, K., Anosike, A., Shah, P. P., Simon, K. M., & Lee, L. K. (2022). Disparities in pediatric mental and behavioral health conditions. Pediatrics, 150(4), e2022058227. https://doi.org/10.1542/peds.2022-058227

Krug, E. G., Dahlberg, L. L., Mercy, J. A., Zwi, A. B., & Lozano, R. (Eds.). (2002). World report on violence and health. World Health Organization.

Lamborn, S. D., Mounts, N. S., Steinberg, L., & Dornbusch, S. M. (1991). Patterns of competence and adjustment among adolescents from authoritative, authoritarian, indulgent, and neglectful families. Child Development, 62(5), 1049–1065. https://doi.org/10.1111/j.1467-8624.1991.tb01588.x

McLanahan, S., & Sandefur, G. (1994). Growing up with a single parent: What hurts, what helps. Harvard University Press.

Merrick, M. T., Ford, D. C., Ports, K. A., & Guinn, A. S. (2018). Prevalence of adverse childhood experiences from the 2011–2014 Behavioral Risk Factor Surveillance System in 23 states. JAMA Pediatrics, 172(11), 1038–1044.

National Child Traumatic Stress Network. (2024). Trauma-Focused Cognitive Behavioral Therapy (TF-CBT). Retrieved from https://www.nctsn.org

National Institute of Mental Health. (2021). Mental illness: Statistics. Retrieved from https://www.nimh.nih.gov

Novaco, R. W. (2011). Anger dysregulation: Driver of violent offending. Journal of Forensic Psychiatry & Psychology, 22(5), 650–668.

Pew Research Center. (2011). A portrait of stepfamilies. Social & Demographic Trends.

Sims, M., Diez-Roux, A. V., Dudley, A., Gebreab, S., Wyatt, S. B., Bruce, M. A., ... & Taylor, H. A. (2012). Perceived discrimination and hypertension among African Americans in the Jackson Heart Study. American Journal of Public Health, 102(S2), S258–S265.

Substance Abuse and Mental Health Services Administration. (2023). National survey on drug use and health: 2023 results. U.S. Department of Health and Human Services.

Sweeney, M. M. (2010). Remarriage and stepfamilies: Strategic sites for family scholarship in the 21st century. Journal of Marriage and Family, 72(3), 667–684.

The Annie E. Casey Foundation. (2022). 2022 KIDS COUNT data book: State trends in child well-being. The Annie E. Casey Foundation.

U.S. Census Bureau. (2023). America's families and living arrangements: 2023 (Current Population Survey Reports, P20-590). U.S. Department of Commerce.

van den Berg, D. P., de Bont, P. A., van der Vleugel, B. M., de Roos, C., de Jongh, A., Van Minnen, A., & van der Gaag, M. (2015). Prolonged exposure vs eye movement desensitization and reprocessing vs waiting list for posttraumatic stress disorder in patients with a psychotic disorder: A randomized clinical trial. JAMA Psychiatry, 72(3), 259–267.

van der Kolk, B. A. (2014). The body keeps the score: Brain, mind, and body in the healing of trauma. Viking.

Wade, R., Shea, J. A., Rubin, D., & Wood, J. (2014). Adverse childhood experiences of low-income urban youth. Pediatrics, 134(1), e13–e20.

Wallace, B. C., & Constantine, M. G. (2005). Afrocentric cultural values, psychological help-seeking attitudes, and self-concealment in African American college students. Journal of Black Psychology, 31(4), 369–385.

Washington, H. A. (2006). Medical apartheid: The dark history of medical experimentation on Black Americans from colonial times to the present. Doubleday.

Woods-Giscombé, C. L. (2010). Superwoman schema: African American women's views on stress, strength, and health. Qualitative Health Research, 20(5), 668–683.

World Health Organization. (2013). Guidelines for the management of conditions specifically related to stress. WHO Press.

World Health Organization. (2019). International classification of diseases 11th revision (ICD-11). World Health Organization.

Yehuda, R., Daskalakis, N. P., Bierer, L. M., Bader, H. N., Klengel, T., Holsboer, F., & Binder, E. B. (2016). Holocaust exposure induced intergenerational effects on FKBP5 methylation. Biological Psychiatry, 80(5), 372–380.

www.ingramcontent.com/pod-product-compliance
Lightning Source LLC
LaVergne TN
LVHW022029200926
848481LV00007B/2616
9798295715402